VIGILANTE DANGER
A Threat to Black Lives

Dr. Artika R. Tyner

Lerner Publications ◆ Minneapolis

Lerner Publications Company
An imprint of Lerner Publishing Group, Inc.
241 First Avenue North
Minneapolis, MN 55401 USA

For reading levels and more information, look up this title at www.lernerbooks.com.

Library of Congress Cataloging-in-Publication Data

Names: Tyner, Artika R., author.
Title: Vigilante danger : a threat to Black lives / Artika R. Tyner.
Description: Minneapolis : Lerner Publications, 2021. | Series: The fight for Black rights | Includes bibliographical references and index. | Audience: Ages 8–12 | Audience: Grades 4–6 | Summary: "The deaths of Trayvon Martin, Ahmaud Arbery, and others have shined a light on the disturbing problem of racism and vigilantism. Explore this modern threat to Black lives and the history of racially motivated attacks"— Provided by publisher.
Identifiers: LCCN 2020041919 (print) | LCCN 2020041920 (ebook) | ISBN 9781728429571 (library binding) | ISBN 9781728430256 (paperback) | ISBN 9781728429656 (ebook)
Subjects: LCSH: African Americans—Crimes against—Juvenile literature. | Racism—United States—Juvenile literature. | Vigilantes—United States—Juvenile literature.
Classification: LCC HV6250.4.E75 T84 2021 (print) | LCC HV6250.4.E75 (ebook) | DDC 362.88089/96073—dc23

LC record available at https://lccn.loc.gov/2020041919
LC ebook record available at https://lccn.loc.gov/2020041920

Manufactured in the United States of America
1 – CG – 12/31/20

Table of Contents

CHAPTER 1

MAJOR
Moments

The family of twenty-five-year-old Ahmaud Arbery said he was jogging in a Georgia neighborhood on February 23, 2020. He was a former high school football star who enjoyed exercising. Two white men, father and son Gregory and Travis McMichael, said they had seen a suspected burglar on a security video near a house that was being constructed. They claimed Arbery looked like the burglar and chased him in their truck.

Both men had guns. Another white man, William Bryan, joined them. The McMichaels hit Arbery with their truck. They then shot and killed him. Bryan recorded the events on his phone.

On May 5, Bryan's video of Arbery's death was leaked on social media. It was shared widely. Due to public outcry, the McMichaels were arrested. They were charged with murder. Bryan was also arrested and charged with murder.

Artist Marvin Weeks said he hoped his mural of Ahmaud Arbery would motivate the Brunswick, Georgia community to come together to discuss racism.

TRAYVON MARTIN

On February 26, 2012, seventeen-year-old Trayvon Martin was walking home after going to the store. He was spotted by a man named George Zimmerman. Zimmerman was a neighborhood watch captain. He called 911 to report Martin as being suspicious.

Trayvon Martin had gone to the store to buy Skittles and soda in the Sanford, Florida, neighborhood where he was visiting his father.

The death of Trayvon Martin and later acquittal of George Zimmerman sparked rallies and protests across the United States.

Zimmerman was told by the dispatcher not to leave his car. Instead, he followed the boy. Then Zimmerman shot and killed Martin. Martin was unarmed.

Following protests, Zimmerman was arrested for second-degree murder. He pled not guilty and was acquitted of the crime. He claimed his actions were based on self-defense. This allows citizens to use deadly force if they fear for their safety.

VIGILANTES IN THE UNITED STATES

A vigilante is a civilian who believes they must take the law into their own hands. Some may believe that a person did not get a harsh enough sentence after committing a crime. So, they take action. It does not matter if their action is legal or not. Even when a crime has not occurred, a vigilante may feel they have a duty to protect themselves or their community. Some may feel they are not safe unless they act.

The Guardian Angels are a vigilante group founded in New York City in 1979. It has spread to 22 US states and 19 other countries.

Many prominent actors, musicians, and professional athletes, such as tennis star Naomi Osaka, have used their public platform to bring awareness of the need for change in the US.

Ahmaud Arbery and Trayvon Martin were seen as suspicious and dangerous. Family members, activists, and others say they have joined the long list of Black victims who have been hurt or killed as a result of vigilantism in the United States.

How can fear lead to violence?

CHAPTER 2

A LOST
History

Lynchings began in the United States in the 1800s. A lynching is a killing committed by a group of people acting outside of the law. Victims of lynchings were most often hanged. Lynchings were often public events. The public gathered to watch the killings.

Vigilantes have used lynchings to intimidate others. After the Civil War (1861–1865), Black people were freed from slavery. Black men were given the right to vote. White supremacists, especially in the South, feared that they would lose social and political power. They created state and local policies to prevent Black men from voting. They also used lynchings to scare the Black community and reinforce white supremacy.

The Ku Klux Klan (KKK) is the oldest hate group in the US. It was founded by Confederate veterans in 1865 to maintain white supremacy. Local communities organized secret meetings. They wore hooded robes. This disguise allowed prominent political figures, police officers, and business leaders to hide as KKK members.

Historians estimate that between 2 and 5 million people were members of the Ku Klux Klan by 1925.

NO JUSTICE

Between 1882 and 1951, nearly 5,000 people were lynched in the United States. The victims were mostly Black. They were labor organizers, business owners, and political activists. These people were killed for rumored involvement with white women, speaking to white people, opening businesses, or trying to vote. Lynching victims were often killed for defending their rights.

Anthony Crawford was lynched in Abbeville, South Carolina, on October 21, 1916. A farmer and businessman, Crawford had disagreed with a white man about a sales price for his crops.

White supremacists often spread rumors that Black people were violent criminals. The rumors were used to justify their actions and make communities fear Black people. Lynch mobs were celebrated for keeping white people safe. The vigilantes in lynch mobs were often never punished.

Walter Francis White

Walter Francis White was born in Atlanta, Georgia, in 1893. His light skin and straight hair allowed him to pass as white. White started a local chapter of the National Association for the Advancement of Colored People (NAACP) and became a national member in 1918. White traveled throughout the South talking to white vigilantes about their role in lynchings. He became a leading member of the NAACP and served as the secretary from 1931 to 1955.

LINGERING BIAS

Although lynchings are no longer common, fear and hatred of Black people still exist. They are often expressed as racial bias.

News media can contribute to racial bias. Black people are shown more often as crime suspects, and white people are more often shown as victims of crime. Multiple studies have shown Black people are overrepresented in crime-related stories. This coverage fuels viewers' fears. It strengthens the connection in their minds between Black people and crime.

Various forms of media, including advertising, television, and movies, often portray Black men as angry individuals who commit crimes.

Racial profiling is the practice of suspecting someone of a crime based on their race. Groups like the American Civil Liberties Union (ACLU) and NAACP have been working to end this practice for many years.

A person may feel that a Black person looks suspicious or dangerous. They may not realize they feel that way because of racial bias. Black people can be hurt or killed when vigilantes act based on their racial biases.

 How is crime reported by your local media? Do you notice racial bias in its reporting?

CHAPTER 3

WEAPONIZING THE **Police**

Vigilantes can use the power of the police to commit violence against Black people. Historically, white supremacists organized patrols to maintain power over enslaved Black people in the South. They punished those who tried to escape or revolt.

During the Civil Rights Movement, racial segregation laws forced Black and white people into separate spaces. Anyone who did not follow the laws was subject to police brutality. They were beaten or attacked by police dogs.

Today, civilians can weaponize the police with what is known as a racial bias call. A person may call the police on someone they find suspicious or threatening. Callers can be influenced by racial bias.

Some US states are trying to make it a crime to call the police due to racial prejudice.

Black students have been attending Yale University since 1870. They make up about 7.5 percent of the student body today.

PERCEIVED THREATS

In 2018, a white student at Yale University called the police on a Black student for resting in a common space. The Black student was questioned by the police. Later that year in Ohio, a white bank teller called the police on a Black man. He was trying to cash his paycheck.

In some cases, people lie when calling the police. In 2020, Christian Cooper was watching birds in Central Park. He asked a white woman, Amy Cooper, to leash her dog. This was a rule at the park. She called the police and lied. She said he was threatening her life. Cooper recorded her call to the police on his cell phone. The video shows that he was not threatening her.

Militarization

Sometimes the police use surplus military equipment. This gear can give officers the appearance of being "at war" with their communities rather than serving them. A recent study showed that militarized police forces are more likely to have violent interactions with the public.

THE RISK OF RACIAL BIAS CALLS

When police respond to racial bias calls, there are a number of risks. It can lead to police brutality or wrongful arrest. A white Starbucks manager called the police on two Black men who were waiting for a business meeting in 2018. The men were arrested. They cooperated with the police.

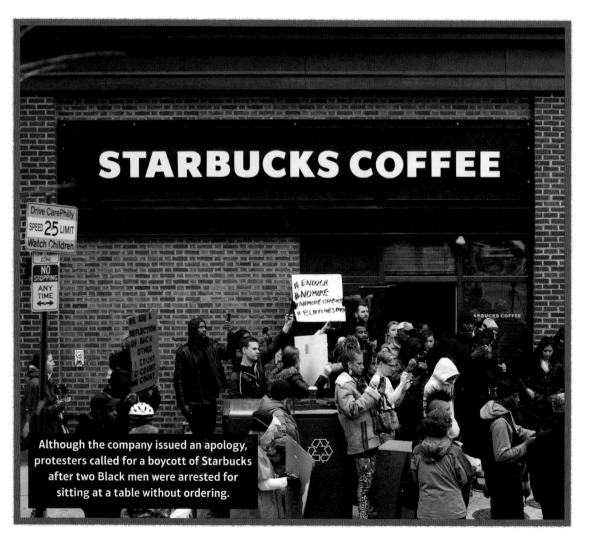

Although the company issued an apology, protesters called for a boycott of Starbucks after two Black men were arrested for sitting at a table without ordering.

The officer who killed Tamir Rice was not fired. Protesters demanded justice for the boy's death.

Not all incidents end peacefully. In 2014, twelve-year-old Tamir Rice was shot by the police. A person had called the police about someone holding a gun in a nearby park. They told the dispatcher that it was probably a kid with a toy gun. But the dispatcher did not tell this to the responding police officers. Within two seconds of arriving on the scene, an officer shot and killed Tamir.

Having bias means you favor some ideas or people over others. Everyone has biases. Identify one of your biases. Why do you think you have that bias?

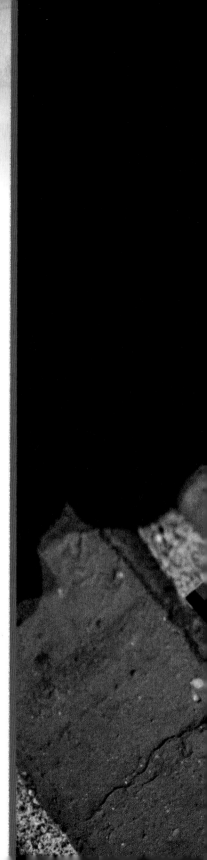

CHAPTER 4

CHANGE COMES
Slowly

In 1955, fourteen-year-old Emmett Till was murdered by two white men. A white woman accused him of whistling at her and flirting with her. Emmett was kidnapped, beaten, shot, and thrown in the river. His killers were found not guilty.

Till's mother insisted on holding an open-casket funeral. She wanted the world to see what vigilantes had done to her son. Till was unrecognizable. *Jet*, a Black magazine, published his photo, and it was republished by mainstream media.

The Black community was outraged by this act of violence against a child. Emmett's murder motivated activists to fight for justice in the Civil Rights Movement.

Emmett Till's killers publicly admitted to their crime after they were found not guilty. They could not be tried for the murder again.

A CAMERA IN EVERY POCKET

Victims and bystanders now use cameras to hold vigilantes accountable. People can record videos of these incidents on their cell phones. The videos serve as evidence of vigilante crimes and bias calls. In the case involving Christian Cooper, video provided the police with key evidence.

Victims have said they do not report racially motivated hate crimes because they are afraid or because they assume law enforcement will not take them seriously.

Sometimes these videos are posted on social media. The videos inspire people to organize protests against racial injustice. They help gather support for legal reforms to protect against discrimination. However, many people argue that these videos can be harmful to Black people who watch them. Black people may see the videos and think that they or their loved ones could be next.

Hate Crimes and the Law

President Barack Obama signed the Matthew Shepard and James Byrd Jr. Hate Crimes Prevention Act into law in 2009. It was named after Matthew Shepard, a gay student, and James Byrd Jr., a Black man. Both men were killed in hate crimes in 1998. A hate crime is when someone is harmed or killed because of their race, sexual orientation, religion, or other identity. The law expanded the definition of hate crimes and removed barriers for prosecuting people who commit these crimes.

VIGILANTE LAWS

Since 1918, nearly two hundred anti-lynching bills have been introduced in Congress. None have passed. The first of these was called the Dyer Anti-Lynching Bill. It intended to make lynching a federal crime. But some senators argued that lynchings were an issue that should be handled by state governments. They blocked the bill from passing.

In 2020, sixty-five years after the murder of Emmett Till, the US House of Representatives passed the Emmett Till Antilynching Act. The bill would make lynching a federal crime and a hate crime. The bill still needs to pass the Senate, which passed a similar measure in 2019.

To protect the lives of Black people, protesters, activists, lawmakers, and the families of victims are working hard to spread awareness and bring an end to racial bias and vigilantism.

The NAACP celebrated its 112th anniversary in 2021. Visit naacp.org. What are one or two issues you're interested in learning more about?

VIGILANTE DANGER
Timeline

February 12, 1909: The NAACP is founded. It is the oldest and largest civil rights organization in the United States.

1931–1955: Walter White serves as the secretary of the NAACP. He investigates lynchings.

August 28, 1955: Emmett Till is lynched in Mississippi after being accused of whistling at and flirting with a white woman.

October 28, 2009: The Matthew Shepard and James Byrd Jr. Hate Crimes Prevention Act is signed into law by President Barack Obama.

February 26, 2012: Trayvon Martin is killed by a neighborhood watch captain.

November 22, 2014: Tamir Rice is shot and killed by the police.

February 23, 2020: Ahmaud Arbery is killed by a father and son.

February 26, 2020: The Emmett Till Antilynching Act is passed by the US House of Representatives.

Glossary

acquittal: when a person is found not guilty of the crime they are charged with

activist: someone who works to make change in the world

bias: an often unfair preference for certain ideas, groups, or individuals over others

dispatcher: a person who receives 911 calls and organizes emergency services

hate crime: a crime motivated by prejudice

lynching: a killing, most often by hanging, of a person by a group without due process

neighborhood watch: a program where people in a neighborhood watch for crimes

police brutality: an act of violence, where police officers use excessive or unnecessary force on a citizen

racial bias: usually negative attitudes, often unconscious, about another race

segregation: the forced separation of different racial groups

self-defense: trying to protect oneself from danger

vigilante: a person who takes law enforcement into their own hands

weaponize: to turn a thing or an action into a weapon

white supremacy: the belief that white people are superior and should dominate other races, like Black people

Learn More

Golio, Gary. *Strange Fruit: Billie Holiday and the Power of a Protest Song*. Minneapolis: Millbrook Press, 2017.

Implicit Bias: Peanut Butter, Jelly, and Racism
https://www.pbs.org/video/pov-implicit-bias-peanut-butter-jelly-and-racism/

Lynching in America: PBS
https://www.pbs.org/wgbh/americanexperience/features/emmett-lynching-america/

Tyner, Dr. Artika R. *Black Lives Matter: From Hashtag to the Streets*. Minneapolis: Lerner Publications, 2021.

Walter White Biography: Biography
https://www.biography.com/activist/walter-white

Weatherford, Carole Boston. *Unspeakable: The Tulsa Race Massacre*. Minneapolis: Carolrhoda Picture Books, 2021.

Index

Photo Acknowledgments

The images in this book are used with the permission of: Sean Rayford/Getty Images, p.5; Allison Joyce/Getty Images, p.6; Spencer Platt/Getty Images, p.7; Michael Loccisano/Getty Images, p.8; Al Bello/Getty Images, p.9; Jack Benton/ Archive Photos/Getty Images, p.11; Library of Congress/Wikimedia, p.12; Hulton Archive/Getty Images, p.13; Paul Bradbury/OJO Images/Getty Images, p.14; rblfmr/ Shutterstock, p.15; Chris Windsor/DigitalVision/Getty Images, p.17; f11photo/ Shutterstock, p.18; Alex Milan Tracy/Sipa USA/Newscom, p.19; Mark Makela/ Getty Images, p.20; Angelo Merendino/Getty Images, p.21; Nathan Howard/Getty Images, p.23; Daniele COSSU/Shutterstock, p.24; Hannes Magerstaedt/Getty Images, p.25; Natasha Moustache/Getty Images, p.27; rosiekeystrokes/Pixabay, background

Cover: Ira Bostic/Shutterstock, left; Regents of the University of California/UCLA, middle; Michael Scott Milner/Shutterstock, right